A Fun Way to Learn to Crochet for Kids

By Rita Weiss and Jean Leinhauser

PRODUCED BY

PRODUCTION TEAM

Creative Directors:	Jean Leinhauser
	and Rita Weiss
Editor:	Susan Lowman
Book Design:	Linda Causee

Diagrams © 2014 by The Creative Partners™LLC

Reproduced by special permission

We have made every effort to ensure that these instructions are accurate and complete. We cannot, however, be responsible for human error, typographical mistakes or variations in individual work.

PUBLISHED BY LEISURE ARTS, INC.

the art of everyday living

© 2014 by Leisure Arts, Inc.

104 Champs Boulevard, STE 100

Maumelle, AR 72113-6738

www. leisurearts.com

ISBN: 978-1-4647-1596-9

Leisure Arts, Inc. • Maumelle, Arkansas

And some of this yarn...

Put these all together and follow our instructions, and you'll soon be a crocheter!

Crocheting is fun and easy to do!

To learn to crochet, all you need are:

Your hands...

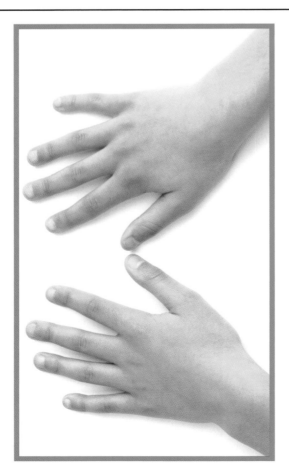

And one of these crochet hooks...

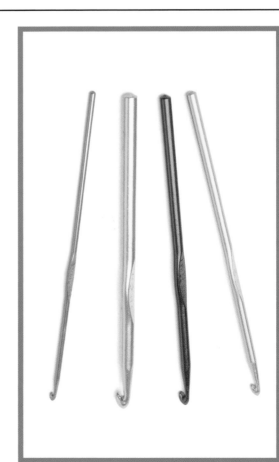

Meet the Hook

Before we begin, let's learn about the hook.

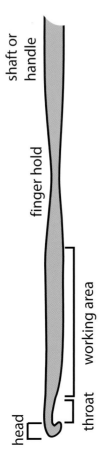

head

throat   working area

finger hold

shaft or handle

The **HEAD**. It will grab (or hook) the yarn and make it easy for you to pull it through to create stitches.

The **THROAT**. This is the slanted area that leads from the head to the working area of the hook. Never work on the throat, or your stitches will be tight; this will make it hard to insert the hook when you crochet the next row.

The **WORKING AREA**. This is the most important part of the hook. Here is where the stitches are formed. Make sure that all your stitches are worked here so they will be the correct size.

The **FINGER HOLD**. Some hooks have an indented space where you can place your thumb to balance your work; some hooks do not. Both kinds work just as well. Just make sure that you never form your stitches on the finger hold, or they will be larger and much too loose.

The **SHAFT** or the **HANDLE**. This is the end of the hook.

How to Hold the Hook

There are two ways to hold the hook: the knife hold or the pencil hold. The choice is yours. Hold the hook in the hand you use for writing.

The **Knife Hold**. Hold the hook just as you hold a knife to cut food.

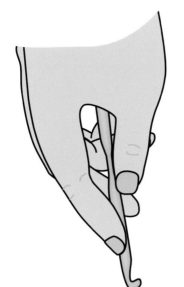

The **Pencil Hold**. Gripping the finger hold area, hold the hook just as you would write with a pen or pencil.

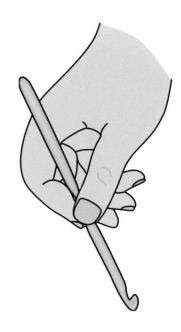

Use whichever type of hold feels most comfortable. There is really no right or wrong way to hold the hook.

The Slip Knot

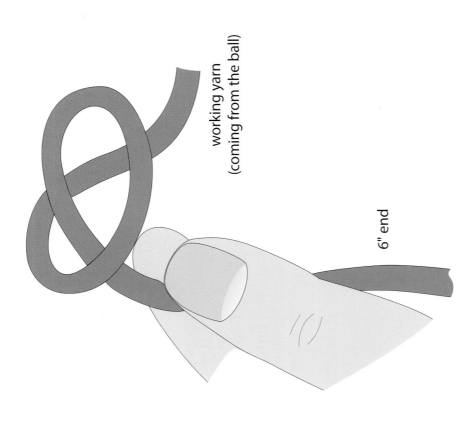

working yarn
(coming from the ball)

6" end

All crochet begins with making a slip knot (sometimes called a slip loop) on the hook. To do this, place the end of the yarn on a flat surface and make a loop as shown, leaving a 6" end.

Now let's get started learning to crochet

You can teach yourself all of the basics of crochet by following this book, where we show it all in pictures.

With your hook and some yarn in your hands, do what the words under each picture tell you to do.

Any time you are not sure that what you are doing is correct, just place your crochet hook on the drawing in the book and check your work by comparing it to the picture.

Before long you will learn all of the basic crochet stitches, and you can practice your new skills on the simple patterns that start on page 27.

Ready for a big adventure?

Set. Get your hook and yarn.

Go! Have fun!

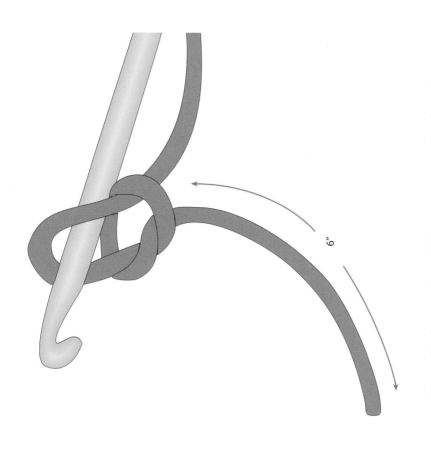

The slip knot should be snug on the hook, but not tight, and should slide easily. Be sure to leave the loose yarn end at least 6" long to use later.

6"

Let's start with a hook made of aluminum or plastic in a size marked "H" or "5 mm." Insert the hook as shown and draw up a loop. Then pull both ends to tighten the loop on the hook.

THE CHAIN STITCH

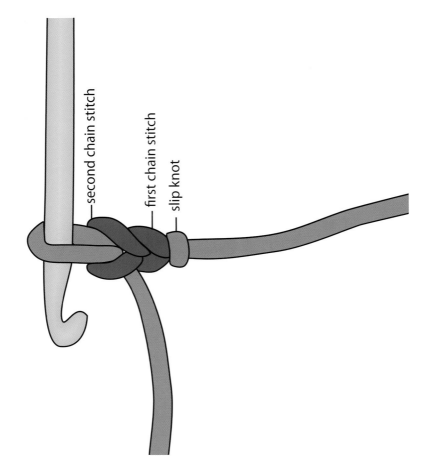

second chain stitch

first chain stitch

slip knot

Once again, take the yarn from back to front over the hook, catch it and draw it through the loop on the hook, which is the first chain stitch you made. You have now made two chain stitches.

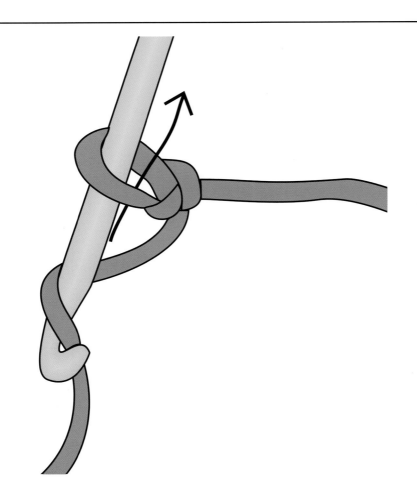

With a slip knot on the hook, take the yarn from back to front over the hook (this is called a "yarn over") and catch it with the hook head. Draw the yarn through the slip knot and up onto the working area of the hook. You have now made one chain stitch.

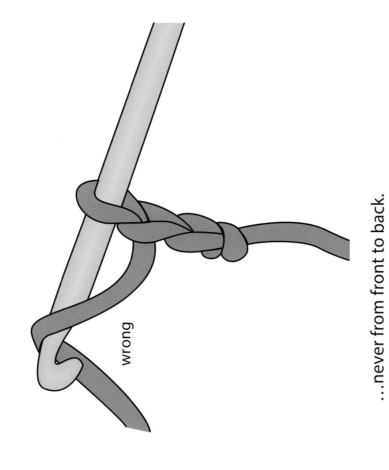

wrong

...never from front to back.

right

TIP: Always take the yarn over the hook from back to front....

Take care to work each stitch only on the working area of the hook.

working area

When counting stitches, never count the slip knot or the loop on the hook.

do not count

1
2
3

do not count

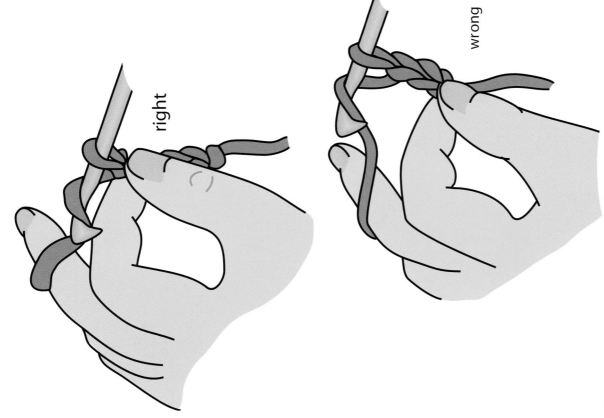

right

wrong

Continue making more chain stitches (we suggest making 10). As you work, keep moving your fingers up closer to the hook after each stitch or two, for better control.

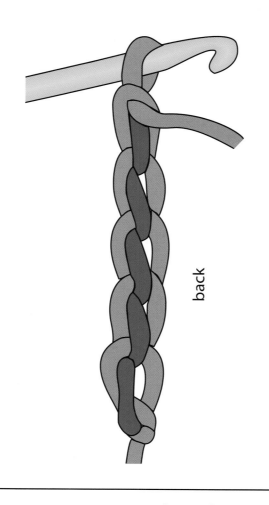

back

The back of the chain has a row of bumps. Each bump also represents one chain stitch. Every V has a bump.

front

The front of the chain stitch will look like a series of V's. Each V stands for one chain stitch.

Step 2: Hook the yarn and draw it through to the front and up onto the working area of the hook.

THE SINGLE CROCHET STITCH

First Row: Right Side

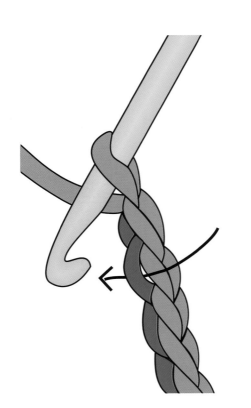

Step 1: Hold the chain with the V side facing you and the row of chain stitches to your left. Skip the first chain stitch and insert the hook from front to back in the back bump of the next chain stitch.

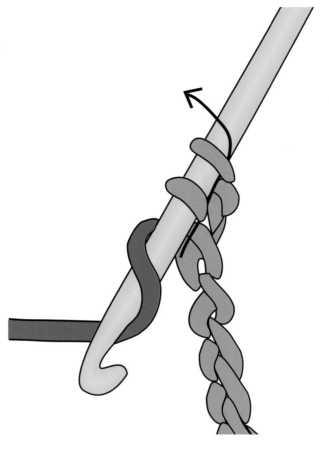

Step 3: Take the yarn over the hook again from back to front, hook it and draw it through both loops on the hook.

There are now two loops on the hook.

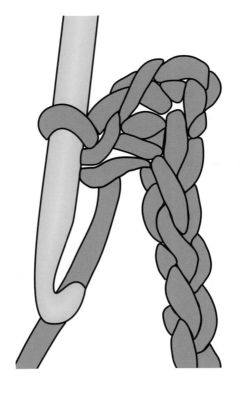

Now insert the hook in the back bump of the next chain stitch and repeat Steps 2 and 3 from pages 10 and 11. You have made another single crochet stitch.

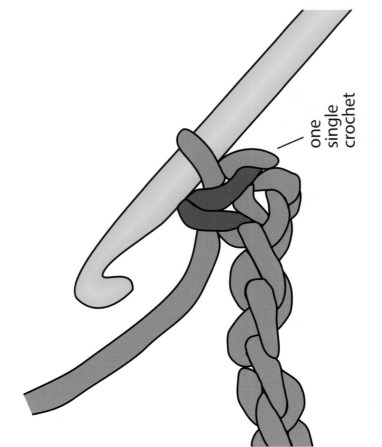

one single crochet

You have made one single crochet! One loop now remains on the hook.

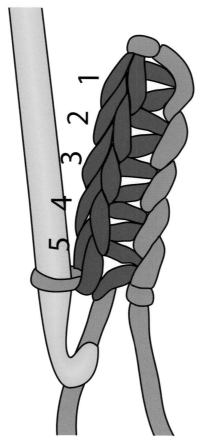

TIP: Remember the loop on the hook is never counted as a stitch.

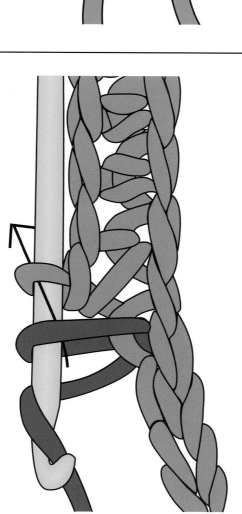

Work in this manner across your row. Take care to work in the last chain stitch but not into the slip knot. If you started with 10 chains, you will have made 9 single crochet stitches, and one loop will still be on the hook.

Second Row: Wrong Side

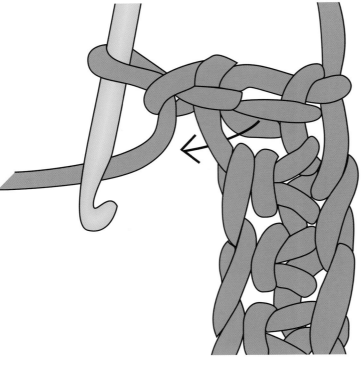

turning chain

turn counterclockwise

Skipping the turning chain, work one single crochet stitch into the single crochet stitch nearest to your hook. You are now going to be working into a stitch—not a chain. Insert the hook from front to back under the top two loops (the V) of the single crochet stitch and repeat Steps 2 and 3 of the first row (see pages 10 and 11). Work one single crochet in each single crochet stitch across the row.

Carefully count your stitches at the end of the row. If you have fewer than on the last row, you may not have worked into the very last stitch.

To work another row of crochet stitches, you first need to bring the yarn up to the correct height to work the first stitch. (Correct height means as tall as your first row of stitches.) This is called the **"turning chain."** For single crochet, you will need to work only one chain stitch. So make one chain stitch and then turn the work counterclockwise.

TIP: Always leave the hook in the work as you turn.

THE DOUBLE CROCHET STITCH

Double crochet stitches are taller than single crochet stitches. To practice making a double crochet stitch, first make a slip knot and then make 14 chain stitches.

First Row: Right Side

Step 1: Bring the yarn over the hook from back to front, then insert the hook in the back bump of the fourth chain stitch from the hook.

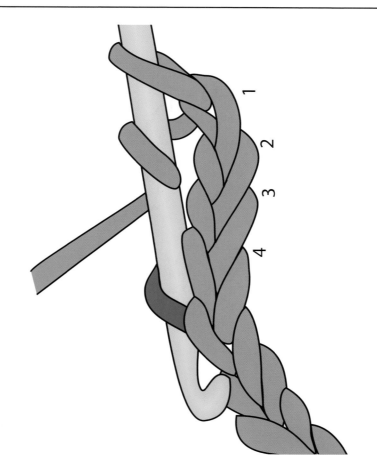

Step 2: Hook the yarn and draw it through the fourth chain stitch and up onto the working area of the hook: there are now 3 loops on the hook.

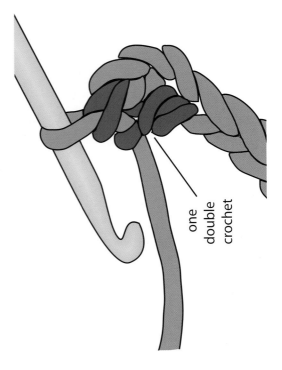

Step 4: Hook the yarn again and draw it through both loops on the hook.

one double crochet

You now have completed one double crochet, and one loop remains on the hook.

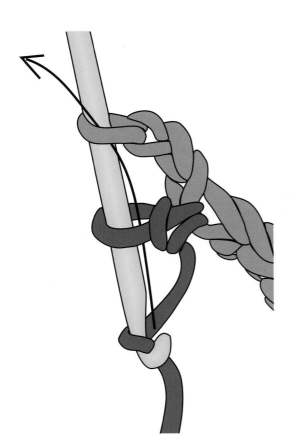

Step 3: Hook the yarn again, and draw it through the first two loops on the hook: there are now 2 loops remaining on the hook.

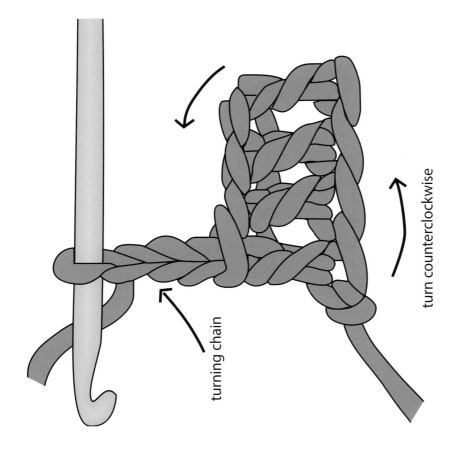

To work the next row, you will again need to work a turning chain (see page 14), and turn the work.

Because the double crochet stitches are taller than single crochet, your turning chain will need to be 3 chains high, to bring the work up to the correct height. Then turn the work counterclockwise as before.

turn counterclockwise

turning chain

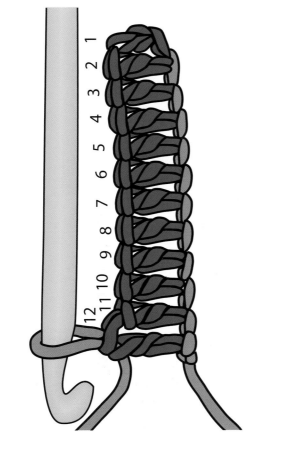

To work the next double crochet stitch, repeat Step 1 (from page 15) but insert the hook into the back bump of the **next** chain stitch rather than in the **fourth** chain stitch from the hook. Then repeat Steps 2 through 4 again (from pages 15 and 16). Continue working double crochet stitches across the whole beginning chain, always working Step 1 into the **next** chain stitch.

Second Row: Wrong Side

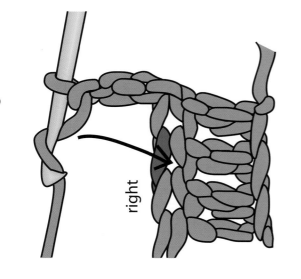

right

The turning chain of 3 chain stitches counts as the first double crochet of the new row. Because of this, you will work your next double crochet in the second double crochet of the previous row. It is very important to place this stitch correctly. The turning chain always counts as the first double crochet of the row. Then the rest of the double crochet stitches are worked into the stitches of the previous row.

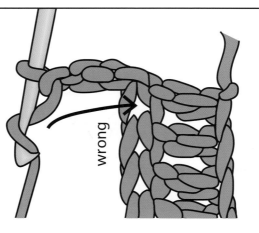

wrong

TIP: Knowing where to insert the hook is sometimes confusing. You must find the top of a given stitch. The V formed by the two loops just to the right of a stitch is the top when working a right-side row, and to the left when working a wrong-side row.

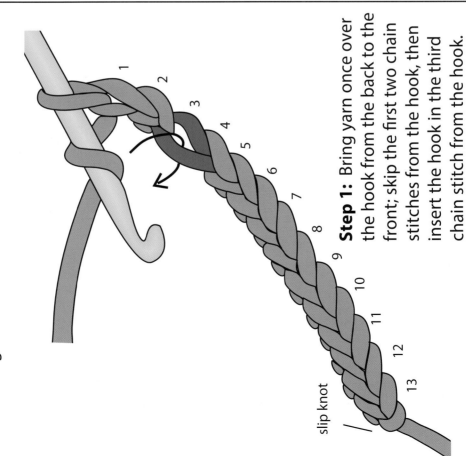

Step 2: Hook the yarn again and draw it through the same chain stitch again and up onto the working area of the hook. You now have three loops on the hook.

THE HALF DOUBLE CROCHET STITCH

As the name says, this stitch is about half as tall as double crochet and eliminates one step of double crochet. To practice making the stitch, first make a slip knot (see page 4) and then make 13 chain stitches (see page 6).

First Row: Right Side

slip knot

Step 1: Bring yarn once over the hook from the back to the front; skip the first two chain stitches from the hook, then insert the hook in the third chain stitch from the hook. (Remember not to count the loop on the hook as a chain stitch.)

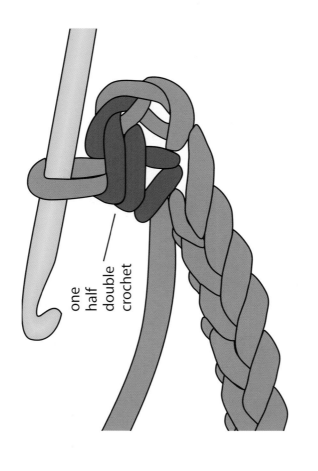

You have now completed one half double crochet stitch, and one loop remains on the hook.

one
half
double
crochet

Step 3: Hook the yarn again and draw it through all three loops on the hook.

Second Row: Wrong Side

Repeat Steps 1, 2 and 3 (from pages 19 and 20) across the row but in Step 1, insert the hook in the **next** half double crochet stitch instead of the **third** chain stitch from the hook.

At the end of the row, chain 2 (for the turning chain) and turn the work counterclockwise. Continue making more rows.

Repeat Steps 1, 2 and 3 (from pages 19 and 20) in each chain stitch across the row, but in Step 1 insert the hook in the **next** chain stitch instead of the **third** chain stitch from the hook.

At the end of the row, you will have one fewer half double crochet stitches than the beginning chain, because you will now count the first 2 chain stitches you skipped at the beginning of the row as one stitch.

Chain 2 and turn the work counterclockwise. The turning chain of 2 chain stitches counts as the first half double crochet of the next row.

THE TRIPLE (TREBLE) CROCHET STITCH

Triple crochet (often called treble crochet) is a tall stitch that works up quickly. To practice making the stitch, first make a slip knot (see page 4) and then make 15 chain stitches (see page 6).

First Row: Right Side

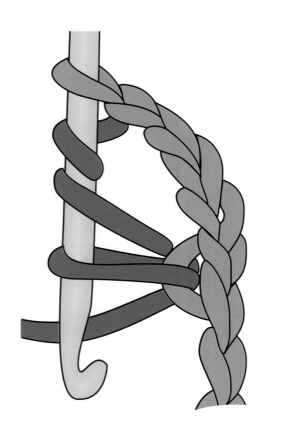

Step 1: Yarn over the hook **twice** by bringing the yarn from back to front over the hook twice. Skip the first four chain stitches from the hook and insert the hook into the back bump of the **fifth** chain stitch from the hook.

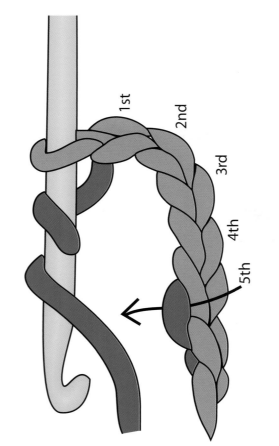

Step 2: Hook the yarn again and draw it through the **same** chain stitch onto the hook; there are now 4 loops on the hook.

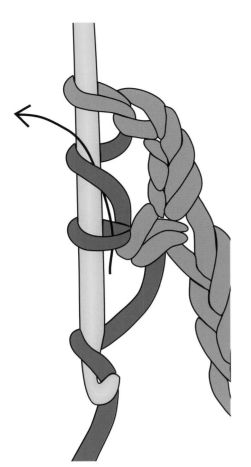

Step 3: Hook the yarn again and draw it through the first two loops on the hook.

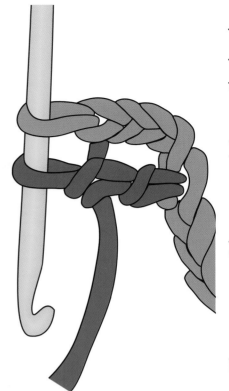

There are now 3 loops remaining on the hook.

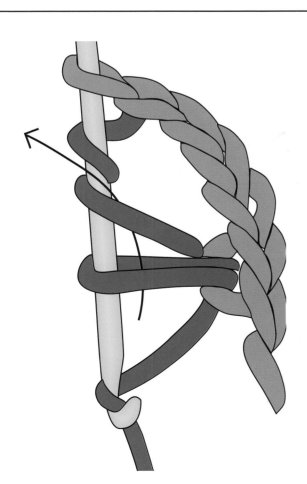

Step 4: Hook the yarn again and draw it through the next 2 loops on the hook.

There are now 2 loops remaining on the hook.

Step 5: Hook the yarn again and draw it through the remaining 2 loops on the hook.

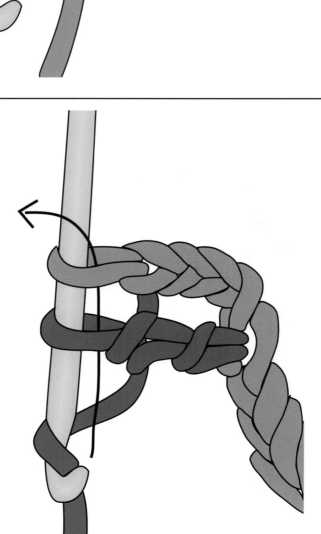

You have now completed one triple (treble) crochet. One loop remains on the hook.

Repeat Steps 1 through 5 (from pages 22, 23 and 24) in the back bump of each chain stitch across the row, working Step 1 in the **next** chain stitch rather than the **fourth** chain stitch from the hook. Chain 4 (for the turning chain) and turn the work counterclockwise.

THE SLIP STITCH

The slip stitch is the shortest of all crochet stitches. It is used mainly to move yarn across an area without adding height. It is also used to join new yarn and to join seams.

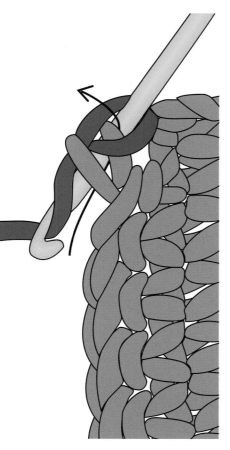

Step 1: Insert the hook in the stitch, chain or loop specified in the project instructions.

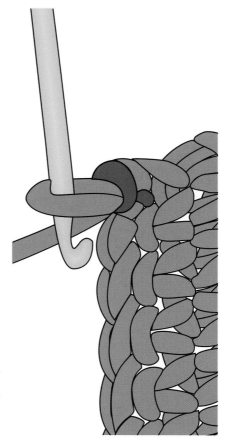

Step 2: Bring the yarn once over the hook from the back to the front and, in one motion, draw the hook through both the stitch, chain or loop and the loop on the hook.

Second Row: Wrong Side

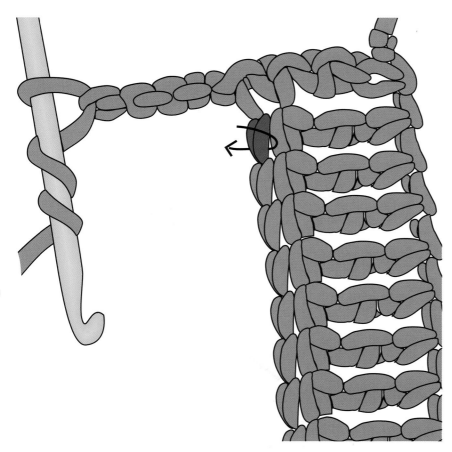

The turning chain of 4 chain stitches has brought your work up to the correct height. Just as in double crochet, the turning chain counts as the first triple crochet stitch of this new row.

So remember to skip the first triple crochet stitch of the previous row and place the next triple crochet stitch in the top of the second triple crochet stitch.

Then repeat Steps 1 through 5 (from pages 22, 23 and 24) in each triple crochet stitch across.

LET'S GET READY TO CROCHET!

Now wouldn't it be fun to make something using the stitches you have learned! On the next few pages you'll find some easy-to-do projects.

Let's start by looking at the instructions for the headband on page 27.

See the skill level listed at the beginning of the pattern. It tells you that this pattern is for beginners. So now you know that you will be able to crochet this pattern. (If you want to know more about skill levels, see page 32, where you'll learn that a beginner is someone who is a first-time crocheter, like you.)

Next check under "Materials" to see what you will need to make the headband. The first item listed is worsted weight yarn, also known as medium weight yarn. Next to it, notice the drawing of a ball of yarn with the number 4. When you buy yarn, look at the ball band (paper label) around the yarn. Find yarn with the number 4 on the ball band, and you have found the correct yarn to use.

Look at what else you will need to make your project. You will, of course, need a crochet hook. You will also need a yarn needle with a large eye and blunt tip. It is used to weave loose ends of yarn into the back of your project after you have finished crocheting it. Thread a loose end of the yarn into the yarn needle and weave it through the backs of your stitches. Never let your needle go through to the front of the project. Weave first in one direction and then in the opposite direction. Trim off any extra yarn.

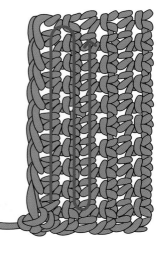

Before the instructions for making the project appear, you see the word "Gauge." This simply means the number of stitches per inch that can be made if you use the yarn and hook size given in the materials list. However, since almost everyone crochets differently—some loosely, some tightly, some in between—the number of stitches per inch can be different even when a crocheter uses the same size hook and the same yarn.

The hook sizes given for any project are only a guide, and they should be checked by first making a gauge swatch.

Here's how you make a swatch to check your gauge. In the list of materials is a crochet hook that is size I/9. The gauge given says that 6 single crochet stitches (worked with the size I/9 hook) will equal 2". Now with the I/9 hook and worsted weight yarn, chain 13 and work in single crochet, with 12 single crochet stitches in each row for about 14 rows. **Finish off** (cut yarn several inches beyond the last stitch worked and pull the yarn end through the last loop remaining on the hook).

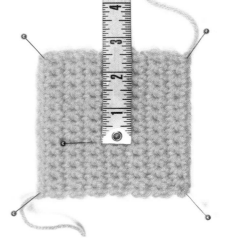

Your finished swatch should be about 4" square. Place your swatch on a padded flat surface and pin it out. Be careful not to stretch the swatch. Measure a 2" area in the center of the swatch and count the stitches per inch.

If you have more stitches than listed in the pattern, try again by making another gauge swatch with a size larger hook (J/10). If you have fewer stitches per inch, make another swatch with a size smaller hook (H/8). Continue making test swatches with other size hooks until your swatch measures the correct gauge.

In a Hurry Headband

In a hurry to try your new skills by making a project? Try this quick-to-make headband. Then when your friends ask you where you got it, you can say proudly, "I made it myself!"

SKILL LEVEL

Beginner ▬ □ □

SIZE

1½" (4 cm) wide x 16" (40.5 cm) long, plus 9½" (24 cm) ties

MATERIALS

Worsted weight yarn

[100% acrylic, 7 ounces, 364 yards (198 grams, 333 meters)] per skein

1 skein red

Note: *Photographed model made with Red Heart® Super Saver® #319 Cherry Red.*

Size I/9 (5.5 mm) crochet hook **or** size required for gauge

Yarn needle

GAUGE

6 single crochets = 2" (5 cm)

INSTRUCTIONS

Chain 51.

Row 1 (right side): Single crochet in second chain stitch from hook and in each remaining chain stitch across; chain 1, turn: 50 single crochets.

Rows 2 through 5: Single crochet in each single crochet across; chain 1, turn. At end of last row, do not chain 1. Finish off (see page 26); weave in ends.

Ties (make 2)

Chain 30. Finish off (see page 26). Weave in one end.

Assembly

Firmly sew remaining end of each tie to center of short edges of headband. Weave in ends.

Sacks for Your Stuff

Do you have a lot of stuff that you carry with you? Then create these cute sacks for your stuff. Make a small one for your cell phone, another one for your game cards. Make a larger sack for your tablet or e-reader. Make some for everyone in your family and for all your friends. As soon as they see yours, they are sure to want at least one.

Cell Phone Sack

SKILL LEVEL

Beginner ▬ ☐ ☐

SIZE

3½" (9 cm) wide x
5½" (14 cm) high

MATERIALS

Worsted weight yarn 4

[100% acrylic, 3 ounces,
164 yards (85 grams,
150 meters)] per skein

1 skein green

Note: *Photographed model made with Caron® Simply Soft® Party™ #0003 Spring Sparkle*

Size H/8 (5 mm) crochet hook **or** size required for gauge

Yarn needle

GAUGE

14 half double crochets = 4" (10 cm); 10 rows = 4" (10 cm)

Notes: *The Sacks are made in one piece, and then folded in half and sewn across the bottom and one side edge. The flap is worked at the top of the piece with half as many stitches as the sack.*

INSTRUCTIONS

Chain 25.

Row 1 (right side): Half double crochet in third chain stitch from hook (skipped chain stitches count as first half double crochet), half double crochet in each remaining chain stitch across; chain 2 (counts as first half double crochet on following row now and throughout), turn: 24 half double crochets.

Row 2: Skip first half double crochet, half double crochet in next half double crochet and in each half double crochet across, working last half double crochet in top of turning chain; chain 2, turn.

Repeat Row 2 until piece measures 3½" (9 cm) high, or for desired height of piece. Do not finish off.

Flap

Row 1: Skip first half double crochet, half double crochet in next 11 half double crochets; chain 2, turn, leaving remaining stitches unworked: 12 half double crochets.

Rows 2 through 5: Skip first half double crochet, half double crochet in next half double crochet and in each half double crochet across; chain 2, turn. At end of last row, do not chain 2. Finish off (see page 26), leaving a long tail for sewing; weave in ends.

Finishing

With right sides together, fold piece in half along the long side. Using tail, sew side edges together and bottom edges together. Weave in all ends. Turn inside out.

Tablet or E-Reader Sack

SKILL LEVEL
Beginner

SIZE
6" (15 cm) wide x 8" (20.5 cm) high

MATERIALS
Worsted weight yarn

[100% acrylic, 3 ounces, 164 yards (85 grams, 150 meters)] per skein

1 skein purple

Note: *Photographed model made with Caron® Simply Soft® Party™ #0006 Purple Sparkle*

Size H/8 (5 mm) crochet hook **or** size required for gauge

Yarn needle

GAUGE
14 half double crochets = 4" (10 cm); 10 rows = 4" (10 cm)

Notes: *The Sacks are made in one piece, and then folded in half and sewn across the bottom and one side edge. The flap is worked at the top of the piece with half as many stitches as the sack.*

INSTRUCTIONS
Chain 43.

Row 1 (right side): Half double crochet in third chain stitch from hook (skipped chain stitches count as first half double crochet), half double crochet in each remaining chain stitch across; chain 2 (counts as first half double crochet on following row now and throughout), turn: 42 half double crochets.

Row 2: Skip first half double crochet, half double crochet in next half double crochet and in each half double crochet across, working last half double crochet in top of turning chain; chain 2, turn.

Repeat Row 2 until piece measures 6" (15 cm) high, or for desired height of piece. Do not finish off.

Flap

Row 1: Skip first half double crochet, half double crochet in next 20 half double crochets; chain 2, turn, leaving remaining half double crochets unworked: 21 half double crochets.

Rows 2 through 7: Skip first half double crochet, half double crochet in next half double crochet and in each half double crochet across; chain 2, turn. At end of last row, do not chain 2. Finish off (see page 26), leaving a long tail for sewing; weave in ends.

Finishing

With right sides together, fold piece in half along the long side. Using tail, sew side edges together and bottom edges together. Weave in all ends. Turn inside out.

29

All Stripes Scarf

The colors in this scarf appear as if by magic because this is a color-changing yarn. So, there's no reason to change colors to create the stripes. Simply work rows of stitches and let the yarn do the striping for you!

SKILL LEVEL

Beginner ◼️▢▢

SIZE

6" (15 cm) wide x 60" (152.5 cm) long

MATERIALS

Worsted weight yarn 🧶 4

[100% acrylic, 3.5 ounces, 280 yards (100 grams, 256 meters) per skein]

1 skein multi-colored

Note: *Photographed model made with Red Heart® Boutique Unforgettable® # 3945 Parrot.*

Size J/10 (6 mm) crochet hook **or** size required for gauge

Yarn needle

GAUGE:

14 double crochets = 4" (10 cm); 7 rows = 4" (10 cm)

INSTRUCTIONS

Chain 22.

Row 1 (right side): Double crochet in fourth chain stitch from hook (skipped chain stitches count as first double crochet), double crochet in each remaining chain stitch across; chain 3 (counts as double crochet on following row now and throughout), turn: 20 double crochets.

Row 2: Skip first double crochet, double crochet in next double crochet and in each double crochet across, working last double crochet in top of turning chain; chain 3, turn.

Repeat Row 2 for desired length, or until you run out of yarn but have a completed row with a long tail for weaving. Finish off (see page 26); weave in ends.

Roll-Up Holder for Your Hooks or Pencils

Designed by Kim Kotary for Red Heart®

Organize your crochet hooks or your favorite pens and pencils in this easy-to-crochet case.

SKILL LEVEL

Easy

SIZE

7" (18 cm) wide x 8½" (21.5 cm) high

MATERIALS

Worsted weight yarn [100% acrylic, 7 ounces, 364 yards (198 grams, 333 meters)] per skein

1 skein turquoise

Note: *Photographed model made with Red Heart® Super Saver® #512 Turqua.*

Size H/8 (5 mm) crochet hook **or** size required for gauge

Safety pins

Yarn needle

GAUGE:

14 single crochets = 4" (10 cm)

Note: *Holder is made in 3 separate pieces; then the pieces are sewn together around the edges and the ties are sewn on the outside.*

INSTRUCTIONS

Outside

Chain 26.

Row 1 (right side): Single crochet in second chain stitch from hook and in each remaining chain stitch across; chain 1, turn: 25 single crochets.

Row 2: Single crochet in first single crochet and in each single crochet across; chain 1, turn.

Repeat Row 2 until piece measures 8½" (21.5 cm) from beginning. Finish off (see page 26); weave in ends.

Top Inside

Make same as Outside, working until piece measures 1½" (4 cm) from beginning. Finish off, leaving a long tail for sewing.

Bottom Inside

Make same as Outside, working until piece measures 4½" (11.5 cm) from beginning. Finish off, leaving a long tail for sewing.

Ties (make 2)

Chain 51.

Row 1: Single crochet in second chain stitch from hook and in each remaining chain stitch across: 50 single crochets. Finish off, weave in ends.

Finishing

Place Outside piece on table. Place Bottom Inside piece on top of it with bottom edges lined up. Place Top Inside piece on top of Outside piece with top edges lined up. Using safety pins, pin together. Using tails, sew outer edges together. Do not sew bottom edge of Top Inside piece and top edge of Bottom Inside piece. Turn assembled piece over and pin Ties to center of Outside piece, approximately 1½" (4 cm) from top edge and 1½" (4 cm) from bottom edge. Sew down center of case through Outside and Inside pieces and Ties. Weave in all ends.

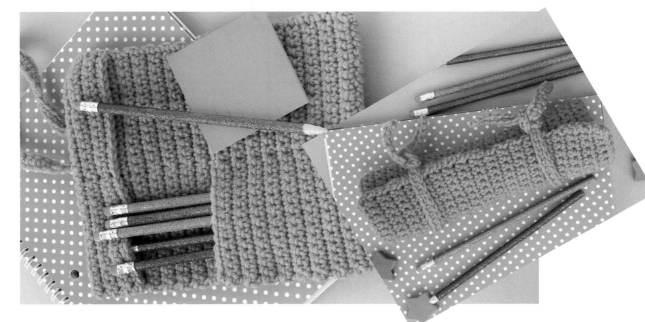

Skill Levels

Yarn manufacturers, publishers, needle and hook manufacturers have worked together to set up a series of guidelines and symbols to bring uniformity to patterns. Before beginning a project, check to see if your skill level is equal to the one listed for the project.

Beginner ▣□□ — Projects for first-time crocheters using basic stitches and minimal shaping.

Easy ▣▣□ — Projects using yarn with basic stitches, repetitive stitch patterns, simple color changes, and simple shaping and finishing.

Intermediate ▣▣▣ — Projects using a variety of techniques, such as basic lace patterns or color patterns, mid-level shaping and finishing.

Experienced ▣▣▣ — Projects with intricate stitch patterns, techniques and dimension, such as non-repeating patterns, multi-color techniques, fine threads, small hooks, detailed shaping and refined finishing.

Standard Yarn Weights

To make it easier for yarn manufacturers, publishers, and designers to prepare consumer-friendly products and for consumers to select the right materials for a project, the following standard yarn weight system has been adopted.

Categories of yarn, gauge, ranges, and recommended hook sizes

Yarn Weight Symbol & Category Names	0 Lace	1 Super Fine	2 Fine	3 Light	4 Medium	5 Bulky	6 Super Bulky
Type of Yarns in Category	Fingering 10 count crochet	Sock, Fingering, Baby	Sport, Baby	DK, Light, Worsted	Worsted, Afghan, Aran	Chunky, Craft, Rug	Bulky, Roving
Crochet Gauge* Ranges in Single Crochet to 4 inch	32-42 sts*	21-32 sts	16-20 sts	12-17 sts	11-14 sts	8-11 sts	5-9 sts
Recommended Hook in Metric Size Range	Steel** 1.6-1.4mm Regular Hook 2.25mm	2.25-3.5mm	3.5-4.5mm	4.5-5.5mm	5.5-6.5mm	6.5-9mm	9mm and larger
Recommended Hook in US Size Range	Steel** 6,7,8	B-1 to E-4	E-4 to 7	7 to I-9	I-9 to K-10.5	K-10.5 to M-13	M-13 and larger

*Lace weight yarns are usually crocheted on larger hooks to create lacy, openwork patterns. Accordingly, a gauge range is difficult to determine. Always follow the gauge stated in your pattern.

** Steel crochet hooks are sized differently from regular hooks—the higher the number, the smaller the hook, which is the reverse of regular hook sizing.

The "Secret" Code for Crochet

Once you have learned to crochet, you will want to find patterns in books and magazines and on the Internet. Crochet patterns, however, are usually written in a special language full of abbreviations, asterisks, parentheses, and symbols and terms. These codes are used so instructions will not take up too much space.

For instance, here are Rows 1 and 2-5 of the Headband instructions on page 27 as they might have been written in the "Crochet Code." They take up much less space than the instructions we have written out in this book.

Row 1(rs): Sc in 2nd ch and in each rem ch across; ch 1; turn: 50 sc.

Rows 2-5: Sc across; ch 1; turn. At end of last row, do not ch 1. Finish off; weave in ends.

These special codes may seem confusing at first, but once you understand them, they are really easy to follow.

Here are some of the more popular abbreviations

beg	begin(ning)
ch(s)	ch(s)
dc	double crochet
hdc	half double crochet
inc	increase
lp(s)	loop(s)
rem	remain(ing)
rep	repeat
rnd(s)	round(s)
sc	single crochet
sk	skip
sl	slip
sl st(s)	slip stitch(es)
sp(s)	space(s)
st(s)	stitch(es)
tog	together
tr	triple crochet
YO	yarn over

Here are some of the more popular symbols

* — An asterisk is used to mark the beginning of some instructions that will be worked more than once, such as "rep from * twice" means after working the instructions once, repeat the instructions following the asterisk twice more (3 times in all).

: — The number after the colon at the end of a row or round shows the number of stitches you should have when the row or round has been completed.

( ) — Parentheses are used to enclose instructions that should be worked the exact number of times spelled out immediately following the parentheses, such as "(ch 3, dc) twice."

[ ] — Brackets and ( ) parentheses are used to provide more information.